FOOTBALL
LEGENDS

RAHEEM STERLING

MUSA OKWONGA

FOOTBALL LEGENDS

RAHEEM STERLING

SCHOLASTIC

Published in the UK by Scholastic Children's Books, 2020
Euston House, 24 Eversholt Street, London, NW1 1DB
A division of Scholastic Limited

London – New York – Toronto – Sydney – Auckland
Mexico City – New Delhi – Hong Kong

Text © Musa Okwonga, 2020
Cover illustration © Stanley Chow, 2020

ISBN 978 14071 9842 2

A CIP catalogue record for this book is available from the British Library.

Printed by CPI Group (UK) Ltd, Croydon, CR0 4YY
Papers used by Scholastic Children's Books are made from
wood grown in sustainable forests.

1 3 5 7 9 10 8 6 4 2

www.scholastic.co.uk

Contents

While this book is based on real people and actual events, some situations and conversations are fictional, created by the author.

LONDON, 2002

Imagine you are sitting high up in a tree, on a sunny Sunday afternoon. There is one small white cloud floating through a bright blue sky, slowly beginning to hide the sun. As you look around, shifting on the branch, you see rows and rows of red rooftops, rolling off in every direction. There is only one building you can see that is taller than the tree where you are sitting. It's a few miles away. It is as high as a block of flats and as wide as a shopping centre, with flags flying from its light grey walls, and two white towers rising above its main entrance. It looks magnificent.

This building is called Wembley Stadium, where the national team of England plays football. You look down from the tree, towards a gap between the houses, at a small square patch of grass. It is then that you see the boy.

He is all alone on the green, and maybe that is why he looks so small. His skin is the colour of the sky just after sunset. He is wearing a red shirt and white shorts, but you can't see what he is wearing on his feet because they are moving too fast. In fact, the boy is moving so fast up and down that patch of grass that at first you think he is flying, even though you know that humans can't do that. He is running after a small white ball. When the ball slows down he nudges it forward with his foot, and every now and then he swerves from side to side, as if he is trying to escape someone who is chasing him. You are so busy watching him that you lean forward too far and you almost fall off your branch.

After a few minutes of running round and round the grass, the boy slows down, and picks up the ball. He gazes at the stadium, which he can just see over the top of the houses. The boy stands there until a woman comes out of the house and calls him to come inside. "Raheem," she says, "dinner is ready," and the boy runs as fast as he did when he was chasing the ball. Raheem, you think, what a lovely name.

KINGSTON, JAMAICA, 1996

Raheem was just two years old, and he had only one parent left.

At the time his dad died, Raheem and his family were living in Kingston, the capital of Jamaica, in an area called Maverley. He was born there, six years after his sister, and it was the kind of place where everyone knew everyone, and where the children always played outside. When there was a storm, the rain would decorate the grey streets, and the children would rush laughing through the puddles; and because the rain was so warm, running in it felt like taking a shower.

People in Raheem's neighbourhood didn't have very much. They had to work hard just so there was enough for everyone. All they really had was their friends and their siblings and their mums and their dads, and some of them didn't even have that.

No one knew exactly what happened to Raheem's dad, but what they did know was that one day some people got very angry with him and went looking for him with their guns. When they found him, they didn't talk, they fired, and that's how they took Raheem's dad away.

It was one of the hardest times in Raheem's life, and it was about to get even harder. Soon his mum had to leave too. She couldn't find a job that paid well enough in Jamaica, so she went to the UK to study there and hopefully earn enough to support her children. Raheem was too young to understand why she had to go. All he knew was that he used to have two parents, and now it felt like he had none.

Surrounded By Love

But even though he had lost his dad forever and his mum had gone far away, Raheem was still surrounded by love. He and his sister went to live with their grandmother.

If he was good Raheem's grandmother would let him go and buy ice cream from the local shop. So many small towns in Jamaica have a shop like that, where it feels like you can buy anything. You normally find them on the corner of a street, and they look very small from the outside, but once you walk inside it's like being in a cave. You just have to tell the shopkeeper what you want, and he'll disappear into a little room at the back for a few seconds before coming out with whatever you asked for. You could ask him for some batteries, a toothbrush, a kettle, even a chicken – just give him a few minutes, and he would return with it in his hands.

That was how Raheem's life started: with some very sad times, but some very happy ones too. Ice cream, running through the rain – and, of course, lots of busy days playing football with his friends. But for him to have a life more exciting than he could imagine, he would have to get on a plane.

DOES THIS COUNTRY HAVE A SUN?

When Raheem was five years old, he and his sister moved to his new home – the city of London, the capital of England. They had gone there to be with their mum, but they soon found that London was very, very different from Jamaica. The buildings were taller and the traffic was louder and the crowds were bigger and, maybe most of all, the weather was colder. Some days he would look up at the sky and ask himself, "Does this country even have a sun?"

Raheem lived in a part of London called Wembley. There were so many people there from all over the world, which meant that at his new school Raheem met children from lots of countries he hadn't heard of before. There were people there from England and India and Sri Lanka and Kenya and Pakistan and Somalia and Ireland and Poland and from Jamaica, just like Raheem. If you walked down the main street and listened carefully, you could hear a new language. If you stopped next to the open door of each restaurant, you could smell a new type of food.

When people met Raheem in his new home they noticed that he didn't talk very much, and they thought he was shy. But he wasn't – he was just getting to know them, working out if he could trust them. When he got to know you well, he talked a lot more.

In View of Greatness

There were plenty of good things about Wembley but there were two that Raheem loved more than anything else. The first thing was that this was the home of Wembley Stadium, the most famous football ground in the world. You could see the stadium from all over the area, and when England were playing, crowds filled the local pubs and people sang songs about their team late into the night, even if they didn't win.

The second thing, of course, was that he was with his mum again. Now he was here, he understood why she had left Jamaica. There were more chances to study in England, and to earn good money. But how he had missed her! He had missed everything about her – the way she laughed and the way she cooked and even the way she said "Raheem!" when she was telling him to stop dashing around the house, because he often knocked things over. Yes – he even missed being told off. And now that his family was back together, now he and his mum and his sister were all sleeping under the same roof, which was all that mattered. When he remembered this, he felt brave enough to do anything.

Wembley Stadium

The Wembley Stadium Raheem loved as a child was knocked down in 2002. A new stadium was built in 2007. It can seat 90,000 people for football matches and is the largest stadium in the UK.

RISE AND SHINE

Beep beep!

Beep beep!

The alarm clock was so loud that it sounded angry. Raheem opened his eyes and groaned at how dark it was – even the sun was still in bed. He looked at the clock. Oh my goodness. 5 a.m.!

"Time to get up, Raheem," said his mum, putting her head round the bedroom door.

"Mum, why are we getting up now?" asked Raheem, rubbing his eyes. "School doesn't start for ages!"

But his mum, who was already dressed in her outdoor clothes, didn't answer him; she had already gone down the corridor. "Hey," he heard her tell his sister, "rise and shine!"

As Raheem dragged himself out of bed, he remembered why his mum had woken him up. *Oh,* he thought, *she needs our help at her job.*

"Don't worry," said his mum, poking her head back round the door, as if she could tell what he was thinking. "I will make sure you get to school on time. I just need you with me for a couple of hours."

Raheem didn't really know what his mum did at work – he knew that she was a cleaner at a hotel in a town near Wembley, a place called Stonebridge, but he had never actually seen her do it. *Well,* he thought, *today I will find out.* He had seen her clean the house before, so maybe it was just like that?

He, his mum and his sister got off the bus and walked up to the front door of the hotel. It was so early that there was no one there except one man sitting behind the reception desk.

"Good morning, Ms Sterling," said the man, smiling at her, then nodding at her children.

"Good morning," said Raheem's mum.

"Good morning," said Raheem's sister.

Raheem looked at the man, and then looked at his mum. He saw that she was smiling at the man, so he nodded at him too, and then he and his family walked upstairs to the first floor.

His mum opened a cupboard and reached inside, taking out two large black T-shirts and a plastic bag. She gave one of the T-shirts to Raheem and one to his sister. "Here you go," she said, "you'll need to put these on." Then she reached into the bag and gave one set of rubber gloves to his sister, and a smaller pair to him. "Same for these," she said. Finally, she took three sponges from the bag, giving them one each and keeping one for herself. She smiled. "Look at us," she said, "a team of cleaners! We're going to be the fastest team that ever did it."

She opened the door of the first hotel room, which was right next to her. "Here we go," she said, pointing inside. "I will replace all of the sheets on the beds, and you and your sister can clean the toilets. You will find the spray under the sink. You don't have to spray too much. There is a brush by the side of the—"

"Wait, Mum," interrupted Raheem. "*The toilets*? Where people – where people do their business?"

"Yes," said his mum.

"Where they go to do a dump?"

"Raheem!" said his sister.

"Urgh," said Raheem. Then he had a worrying thought. "Mum," he asked, "are we going to clean every single room on this floor?"

"Yes."

"And every single room has a toilet?"

"Yes."

Raheem looked out of the door and down the corridor, which seemed to go on forever.

"We are never going to get out of here."

But it wasn't so bad in the end. Raheem's mum was right – after listening to her instructions, they were quick, very quick, because they learned fast and because she promised them any food they wanted from the vending machine. When they were finished, Raheem would race his sister to the machine – she would sometimes beat him, but only if she started running before he did. Then they would get a bar of chocolate as well as a sweet drink, and wait for their mum as she got changed out of her hotel clothes, and got dressed for another one of her jobs.

Their mum was always working, working, working. Some days she came home and she was so tired she would just sit quietly on the sofa for a long while. That's why Raheem and his sister, even though they didn't like cleaning the toilets, didn't mind it as much after a while. It meant that at least they were with their mum – that at least she wasn't alone.

OCTOPUS

There were many days when Raheem felt as if his brain was a giant television and the only programme playing on it was football.

Each time, he was the commentator, but the match on the television was always different. Sometimes it was him and his friends kicking about in the local park:

"And young Sterling has the ball, out on the right. Goes past Dave, goes past Imran. Looks up, there's John in the box. He hits the cross – John leaps – what a header, Ash dives but can't reach it! What a goal that was! The crowd goes wild! So far they have been playing for four hours and the score is Raheem's Dream Team 94, Wayne's Wanderer's 94! It's yet another epic game in the Wembley Champions League!"

Matches like these didn't have much of an audience – it was only the local park, after all. The only people who normally saw these games were people walking past with their dogs, but they did get excited whenever someone scored, and sometimes the dogs even tried to join in. On those days, it didn't matter if it was raining, the games only stopped when it was so dark they couldn't see the ball any more.

Other times, the match playing in Raheem's brain was the type you would find on real television, one of those games on a Wednesday evening where there are tens of thousands of fans in the stadium and the floodlights are as bright as stars. Today, the match was Manchester United against Barcelona, at Old Trafford, and it was just about to begin. The home supporters roared as the players jogged on to the pitch, the referee checked his watch and put his whistle to his lips—

"Raheem!"

Who was shouting at him, trying to interrupt his programme? Raheem turned up the volume in his head, so that the crowd was louder than the voice calling his name. "*United*," sang the crowd. "*United!*"

"Raheem!'

Oh no! The television in Raheem's head turned off, the screen went black, and suddenly he was in a classroom, and everyone was looking at him. Everyone – including his teacher.

"Raheem! Were you paying attention?" she asked.

What could he say? He couldn't tell her that he had been thinking about football instead of concentrating on his lesson.

"Yes!" he answered. "Yes, of course!"

"So what was the answer to my question?"

"Octopus."

The entire class burst out laughing.

"Octopus. That's your answer?"

"Yes."

"Octopus," said his teacher, walking back to the blackboard. "Very good," she says. "I asked, 'What is the capital of Belgium?' and Raheem replied, '*Octopus*.'"

"Oh," said Raheem, and the class laughed some more.

After the class, Raheem went to his teacher.

"I am sorry I wasn't paying attention, Miss," he said. "I didn't mean to get distracted."

"You never do," said his teacher. "Listen, Raheem. You are a clever student, but your brain is always somewhere else." She shook her head. "I am going to ask you a question, and you have to tell me the truth. Promise?"

"Promise," said Raheem.

"When you get distracted like that, is the answer always football?"

"Yes," said Raheem. "Yes, it is."

"Raheem," said his teacher, "I am very sorry, but you can't keep going through school thinking about one thing when the rest of the class is working on another."

"I'm sorry too, Miss."

"This has happened too many times," she said.

Oh no, thought Raheem. *That doesn't sound good.*

"We are going to have to put you under special supervision," his teacher said.

That sounded even worse.

"Special supervision," his teacher said, "is for students who don't work hard enough, and so the school has to keep an extra eye on them. So we are going to take you out of this big class and put you in a small class. Only six students, and three teachers. You can't play around or get distracted in there."

Raheem wanted to disagree but he could see from the look on his teacher's face that there was no point in complaining. He was just worried about what he was going to tell his mum.

When she found out, she was very disappointed, which made Raheem sadder than if she had been angry. Raheem wanted to make his mum proud, so he worked so hard that after a year he moved back to the big class, and he didn't get in trouble at school again.

CLIVE ELLINGTON

Raheem was quiet around most people, but this man was special. The local parents loved him. His name was Clive Ellington. Raheem saw him every weekend at the local youth club. When he spoke, he had a soft, gentle voice, as if there was a sleeping baby nearby and he was trying not to disturb it. When he smiled, his teeth shone like tall chalk cliffs on a sunny day. But maybe the best thing about Clive was his eyes. Some people have eyes that can talk, and when Clive was listening to you his large brown eyes always said the same thing: "You can trust me. You are safe here. I am not going to look away until you finish everything that you need to say."

Clive would spend plenty of time with children in the neighbourhood like Raheem, those who were growing up without their dads, because he knew that life could be very hard for them. Sometimes he would take them around the city, far away from Wembley, because there were so many exciting places in London to discover. Other times he would just sit with them and hang out. Whatever Clive did, he wanted each of the children to be happy, and that's why he decided to have a chat with Raheem.

"Raheem," Clive asked him, "what do you love to do?"

Of course, if you had looked at the television inside Raheem's head, you would have found a programme about football, the same way that if you looked inside a dog's head you would find a programme about bones. But no one had asked Raheem what he loved, because not many people asked eight-year-old children things like that, but Clive was different.

And Raheem gave the only answer that he could: "I love playing football."

When Clive heard that, he was very pleased, for two reasons. First, because he had seen Raheem kicking a ball against a wall, and just from that he knew he was good. Secondly, because he coached a football team which played every Sunday, and so he asked Raheem to play for them. Joyfully, Raheem agreed, and with the permission of his mum he became a member of the first football club of his career: Alpha and Omega FC. It would turn out to be the perfect name. Alpha means "the beginning" and Omega means "the end"; and for Raheem, his new team was the end of an old life, before he had met Clive, and the beginning of a new one, when the world would start to find out just how gifted he really was.

FOOTBALL LEGENDS

ONE HUNDRED
PER CENT

As Raheem walked towards his first training session with Clive's football team, he felt a little bit nervous. His stomach was jumping about, the same way it does when your car goes too fast over speed bumps.

What was he worried for? He knew he was very good at football. He played it all day in the holidays, and he would have played it all night if he didn't have to go to bed. So why was he afraid?

As he stepped into the changing room at the training centre, he knew why: because until now he had always played football for fun, and this was the first time in his life that playing football felt like an exam. He hoped that he would pass.

All the other boys in the changing room knew each other. They talked loudly, throwing jokes and clothes at each other, and they didn't notice Raheem at first, who had sat in the corner of the room nearest the door and was slowly unfolding his clothes.

They only really saw him when they were running out on to the pitch, and they each offered him a smile of encouragement as they jogged past.

"Good luck, mate!" yelled one boy, with a friendly wink. "First day at school, eh?"

"Heard about you from Clive," said another one of them, who Raheem later learned was the team captain. "Can't wait to see you play. Hope you get a goal today." He patted Raheem on the shoulder, and before Raheem could thank him he was already gone.

Raheem was the last out on to the grass pitch, which had two low and wide sets of goalposts, the type you used for seven-a-side football. Clive was standing in the middle of the group of boys, talking and looking very serious, but as soon as he caught sight of Raheem his mouth widened into a large grin.

"Glad you could make it, Raheem!" said Clive.

"We'll do some running with and without the ball, then some skills practice, then finish up the session with a game. Does that sound good to you?"

Raheem gave Clive a thumbs-up. "That's perfect," he said, and then he put his hands on his stomach. All the jumping had gone.

Rocket Raheem!

"Let's go for a run first," said Clive, standing at the edge of the pitch. "When I say go, you sprint. Go!"

And Raheem went.

He only stopped when he realized that Clive had not called him to stop and so he turned around and looked back at where he had come from. There, maybe twenty metres behind him, was everyone else. All the boys looked shocked, but Clive was just laughing.

"What on earth was that?" said the captain, confused.

"He's got rockets in his boots," said the boy who told him it was his first day at school. "Rocket Raheem!"

Clive then asked the boys to stand in a circle and gave them each a football, so that they could each keep it in the air as long as they could – an exercise that was called "juggling". "Left foot, right foot, head, doesn't matter," said Clive. The boys all started to juggle, but one by one their footballs started misbehaving, bouncing off their shins and knees and rolling away across the grass.

"I did forty-one," said one boy proudly. "Better than last time."

"I only did seventeen," said another sullenly. "Rubbish."

Then they eventually all looked at Raheem, who was muttering under his breath:

"One hundred and twenty-five. One hundred and twenty-six."

Raheem's football was behaving itself perfectly, doing exactly what Raheem's feet told it to do. It was floating from his left boot to his right boot and it was spinning so quickly that you couldn't read the writing on the logo.

"Wow," said the captain.

By end of the training session, the other boys were impatient to see Raheem play. Half of them were given blue shirts, and to Raheem's delight he was given a red shirt – the colour of the team he supported, Manchester United.

"Ah." The boy who had gently teased Raheem about being new at school looked down at the blue shirt in his hands. He had just realized that he was marking Raheem.

Clive put his whistle to his lips. "Ten minutes each way," he said. "Let's see what you boys have got."

Just two minutes into the game, Raheem got the ball, out on the right side of the pitch, and about twenty yards from goal. His opponents had already seen how fast he was, so they didn't run towards him. Instead, they stayed back so that he couldn't sprint past them, which seemed like a sensible thing to do.

Raheem put his head down and thrashed the ball so hard with his right foot that before anyone could move it was already bouncing out of the net.

This time, no one said anything. But when Raheem looked up, he saw them all standing in a circle around him, and every one of them was clapping. He looked up at the trees next to the pitch, where he saw two birds flapping their wings. Even they seemed to be applauding him.

If football was an exam, then he had just passed with a score of one hundred per cent.

ALPHA AND OMEGA

The only thing that changed about Raheem was the size of the crowd watching him play. At first, it was just a single bird high up in a tree, looking down as he floated across the grass of a Wembley courtyard. Then it was Clive and Raheem's teammates at Alpha and Omega, shaking their heads in amazement as they saw him in that first training session. Now it was scouts from some of the biggest clubs in the city, who stood by the side of the pitch as Raheem ran past. Each year there were more of them, from all over London, jumping in their cars or on to trains from Fulham and White City and Islington whenever they heard he would be playing. And every time they came to see him, the scouts got more and more excited, because the best thing about Raheem was not his speed, or his skill, or his strength, but his resilience. He just never gave up. He didn't care what the weather was like – whether it was one of those rare summer days where it was too hot for most people to stay outside, or if the pitch was covered in ice or thick with mud. It didn't matter if defenders knocked into him so hard that he flew up in the air. He just kept running, kept shooting, kept scoring.

Scouts

Clubs send out scouts to find new and emerging talent, often from local junior teams. The main job of the scout is to attend matches and find players that they think might make a positive new addition to a team. When a scout spots a player they think has potential, they make a recommendation to the club, and the academy coaches might invite that player to a trial to test their skills. The trials are an important step and help coaches work out if a player has a good technique and suitable personality that will fit in with the existing team. An important role for a scout is to find players that can fill key gaps in a club's line-up to make a great team even greater.

Soon, many people started to know Raheem's name, not just children in his class at school but some of the older boys in the higher years. They would come up to him in the corridor, a group of them, and say, "Hey, Raheem." He would nod back at them. Some of the girls in his year would come up to him and say, "Hey, Raheem," too, but the way they said it was different to the boys, and Raheem found it harder to nod back at them.

But he didn't really care very much about any of that. Not compared to how much he cared about football, football, football. And the scouts saw it too. A few of them got so excited about him that they even asked Clive if they could speak with Raheem's mum, to see if he would be interested in playing for their teams. When Raheem found out who was interested, he couldn't believe it.

"Arsenal! Arsenal!" he told his school friends. "Arsenal want to sign me!" This was incredible. He was going to go to work and sit in the same canteen as Arsène Wenger and Patrick Vieira and Thierry Henry!

Start from the Bottom

But his mum had other ideas.

"Raheem, I don't think you should go to Arsenal," she said one afternoon."

"But Mum it's my dream!" insisted Raheem.

"No it's not," she said. "Your dream is to become a footballer."

Raheem looked confused. "But doesn't that mean playing for Arsenal?" he asked.

"Look at it this way. You are brilliant at football. Maybe the best young footballer in your school, and in the whole of Wembley. But is London much bigger than Wembley?"

"Yes," said Raheem. He didn't understand where

she was going with this.

"And is the UK much bigger than London?"

"Yes," said Raheem. He *still* didn't understand where she was going with this.

"And have you ever met any footballers as good as you?"

Raheem thought about it. There was that left-back the other week, and that striker. Oh, and that goalkeeper somewhere in South London – Streatham? – was amazing.

"Yes," he admitted reluctantly.

"Okay. Now imagine how many brilliant young boys all over London and all over the country want to play for Arsenal. And look at Arsenal. They buy people from all over the world! So if you sign for Arsenal, you're going to turn up for training on your first day, and all of them are going to be just as good as you. And it's going to be so hard for you to stand out."

"Oh," said Raheem. His mum had a way of not only saying things he didn't expect but making him understand at once that she was right. It was a weird kind of magic. "But what should I do?"

"Go to QPR," she said.

"QPR!" exclaimed Raheem. He was shocked. He didn't know anyone who supported Queens Park Rangers. Not one! The only time he heard people talk about QPR was when they were making fun of them. What was that song that boy in the playground sang about them? "Quarter Pound of Rubbish!"

Queens Park Rangers

Club name: Queens Park Rangers Football Club
Nicknames: Rangers, The Super Hoops
Founded: 1882
Current manager: Mark Warburton
Current league: Championship League
Emblem: A circular emblem with the club's initials

"Yes," she said. "They are a smaller club than Arsenal, so they won't have as many Raheems. And they will be able to pay more attention to you and to your career. You'll be able to start from the bottom, and build yourself up."

Why would I want to start from the bottom? That will never work, thought Raheem. Then he looked at his mum and remembered how she had started from the bottom in England, and what she had managed to do. Look how happy they were now.

"Okay, Mum," he said. "Let's do it."

THREE BUSES

In life, people will often tell you to do what makes you happy, to follow your dream. The problem is that sometimes your dream is very far away.

Raheem's dream was very, very far away – three buses away, to be exact. Although he lived in Wembley, the training ground of his new football club was over in Heathrow, not far from the airport. To get to QPR's training ground, Raheem had to travel all the way from the north-west of London, through the suburbs and along a motorway. Because it was such a long distance, his mum wouldn't let him go by himself. Instead, she always sent him with his sister.

It took eight hours every day – the trip from school to the QPR ground and then training at QPR and then the trip all the way back. After Raheem had done a full day of school, he and his sister would walk, a little tired, to the first of the three bus stops. They would set off at 3 p.m. and climb to the top of the double-decker bus, peering over the tops of the trees and the houses as they went past. Sometimes they chatted about their day; sometimes they both got some rest. When they arrived at QPR's training ground, Raheem's sister waited for him in the canteen, and afterwards they began the long journey home. They did this all through the summer and the winter for years, and no matter how exhausted his sister was, Raheem never, ever heard her complain. Just being with him was one of the most quiet but powerful acts of love she could have shown him, and Raheem would always be grateful for it.

LIVERPOOL IS
VERY FAR AWAY

Raheem was having a great time at QPR. He was
learning so fast that they put him in teams to train
with much older footballers. Even though he was still
only fifteen, he was playing against adults. He had
played his first game for England, for QPR's Under-
16s team, and it had even been shown on television.
He had come on just before the end of the first half,
with the score 0–0, and had helped to create both
of his team's goals as they went on to a 2–0 win. In
fact, Raheem was doing so well at QPR that one day
he came home with good news and bad news.

"Hey, Mum," said Raheem, asking her to take a

seat in the living room. "I've got something exciting to tell you."

At once, his mum was worried. Raheem didn't seem excited. He sounded happy, but his eyes looked sad.

"It's Liverpool," he said. "They want to sign me." He paused. "And I want to go."

"Oh that's amazing news! Well done, Raheem!" said his mum. She was so glad for her son – this was what he deserved. This was brilliant for Raheem. This was Liverpool! One of the most famous clubs in the world. They had been champions of England eighteen times. They had been champions of the whole of Europe five times. And Raheem had worked so hard on his game that she was sure he would do well there. He wasn't just another very good player any more – now everyone knew he was special.

But his mum also knew why Raheem's eyes were sad. It was hard for her, but she had to say what they were both thinking.

"Liverpool is very far away," she said, frowning.

"I know," said Raheem. He had looked at the map of England and the distance between London and Liverpool seemed to go on forever.

"It's about three hours," said his mum. Raheem knew what that meant. If he travelled all the way up to Liverpool and back every day he would be exhausted by the end of the week.

"Mum, I think I will have to move there," said Raheem.

They were quiet for a while. It was strange how life could go. A few years ago, his mum had to leave Raheem behind and travel far away so that she could make a better life for the family. And now it was Raheem who would have to leave his mum behind, and his sister, and everything he knew.

"It's a good thing, though, Mum," said Raheem. "Look at how things are here. I love it in Wembley but it's been getting rough round here recently. It will be good for me to get away, I think. If I go up to Liverpool I can just block everything else out and concentrate on football."

Raheem's mum listened. Though she was still upset, she was so proud of him. She had never heard him sound so confident, so determined.

"I'm going to do it, Mum," Raheem said. "I'm going to go up there and I'm going to make it, for all of us."

"I know you will, Raheem," said his mum. "I know you will." She smiled, and tried not to think of the day when he would first take that long train journey up north.

Liverpool

Club name: Liverpool Football Club
Nickname: The Reds
Founded: 1892
Current manager: Jürgen Klopp
Current league: Premier League
Emblem: The Liver Bird, an imaginary cross between an eagle and a cormorant, with the words 'You'll never walk alone.'

EAT, FOOTBALL, SLEEP

From the moment Raheem arrived in Liverpool in early 2010, he was ready to get down to some serious work. His new club had found him a very peaceful place to stay – in a house with a very friendly elderly couple, who treated him as well as his grandmother had back in Jamaica. Every day they would make him breakfast, and then he would go off to work. He would speak to his mum regularly on the phone, and she would always remind him to ask God for a little bit of extra help. When he was in London, during his short holidays from training, he would only see a few people – his mum and his sister, of course, and also a girl he had started dating. Otherwise, for the next two years, that was Raheem's mostly simple routine: eat, football, sleep, eat, football, sleep. Up in Liverpool, and away for his family for the first time, he did not always stay out of trouble, but he made sure to keep working on his dream.

Soon, more and more people around the club started talking about him. Who, they asked, was this new boy from London, who was very quiet but who, when you gave him the ball, was faster than anyone? Where did he learn to play like that? One evening at Anfield, which was Liverpool's home ground, Raheem played in a cup game for the youth team, against Southend United. Liverpool won 9–0, and Raheem scored five goals. Each time he ran at the defenders, they looked scared, stepping away from him because they were worried he would run past them – and, each time, he thrashed the ball into the corner of the net. Up in the crowd that night was Kenny Dalglish, one of the greatest players and managers in Liverpool's history. He had seen many amazing footballers come to Anfield, and it looked like Raheem was another one of them. Sky Sports even wrote an article about his outstanding performance, and Raheem's reputation grew and grew. A year later, in March 2012, he became one of the youngest ever people to play for Liverpool's first team; and that was when someone very important came calling.

PROUD TEACHERS

England's football team had a friendly match against Sweden coming up in November 2012, and England's manager, Roy Hodgson, had an announcement to make. "I will use the November game in Sweden to look at a few players," he told the journalists. One of them, he said, would be Raheem.

This was Raheem's moment. He had worked so hard for this day, when he would finally jog on to the pitch wearing that famous white shirt with three lions on its badge. His mum and his sister were so proud of him. They all had thought Roy Hodgson might want to ask him, because he had been playing so well for Liverpool. But now that it was really happening, they were full of joy.

Raheem was too. He played from the start of the game, and though England lost 4–2 – with the brilliant Zlatan Ibrahimović scoring all four of the Swedish goals – it didn't really matter, in the end. What mattered was that he was an England player.

In 2014, another landmark moment came for Raheem when he played for England at Wembley for the first time, in a friendly against Denmark. It was great to play for England, but it was even more special to play for them at home, in front of so many fans. One of the best things, too, was the ride in the coach on the way to the game. Raheem looked out of the window at his neighbourhood, remembering his friends. He tried to spot the houses where some of them used to live. It was like watching a movie of his life. As he walked out to play, he wondered how many of his friends were watching him now, in the crowd or on television in the pub or at home. At the end of the game, which England won 1–0, Raheem was named man of the match. Maybe some of his old teachers were watching him too. Maybe they were very proud.

A VERY
CUNNING MAN

The last time Liverpool won the league championship had been in 1990 – four years before Raheem was even born. In 2013, though, they had an excellent team, who played fast and entertaining football. They had five players who could attack as well as anyone in the Premier League. There was their superstar midfielder, Steven Gerrard, who had played hundreds of times for Liverpool and who had won them the Champions League. Some said he was the second-best footballer who had ever played for Liverpool, behind Kenny Dalglish. There was Philippe Coutinho, from Brazil. When Coutinho got the ball, you couldn't tackle him, it was like trying to grab a ghost. There was Luis Suárez, the Uruguayan striker who scored a goal nearly every single game. There was Daniel Sturridge, who had strength, speed and skill like almost no one else. And, of course, there was Raheem.

Raheem was playing out on the wing, and whenever he got the ball the crowd gasped, because they knew what was coming. You know when you watch someone skiing down a mountain, going faster and faster as they move over the slope, swerving from side to side, and it seems like nothing can stop them? That's what it was like watching Raheem running with the ball. One second, he was surrounded by defenders: and then, the next second, he was so speedy that he was all alone.

A Winning Team

At the beginning of the 2013–14 season, Liverpool's fans were not expecting too much. But then they saw the way that Brendan Rodgers, their very talented manager, had coached the team to play, and they started to dream that their club could do something special. When Liverpool attacked, it was like watching a fire rush through a forest. They were just so quick, so passionate, so relentless.

When December came, halfway through the season, Liverpool were nearly top of the league, not far behind Manchester City and Chelsea. And then the excitement really began – because Liverpool just kept on winning, winning, winning. The victories kept coming:

Liverpool 4, Everton 0!

Liverpool 5, Arsenal 1!

Liverpool 3, Manchester United 0!

Liverpool 6, Cardiff City 3!

Liverpool 4, Tottenham Hotspur 0!

The crowd at Anfield was amazing, cheering them on every minute. They would start singing long before the game, and they would chant and shout all the way all through the match. There were forty-five thousand people in the stadium, but they were so loud that sometimes it seemed as if you could hear a million voices.

Every Monday, when people in Liverpool went back to work and back to school, they would talk about what Raheem and his teammates were doing.

In their offices, playgrounds, hairdressers and barbershops, they would discuss the latest goals and scores. When they were in the queues at the supermarket or on the bus home, strangers would start conversations with each other about the games:

"Did you see that match! We were four goals up after half an hour!"

"Right? I've not seen us play like this in years! We are looking top-drawer out there. We just need to let in fewer goals."

"Stevie Gerrard is looking better than ever! You wouldn't think he was getting older. He's running around like a kid!"

"I agree. We're absolute class! We just need to play a bit calmer at times. Stop dashing round at a hundred miles an hour."

"Very true. And what about that lad Raheem Sterling? Two goals against Norwich? He's a real player."

"Two goals against Arsenal too, and he's only a teenager! He is coming on nicely, young Raheem. Can't wait till the next game."

Highs and Lows

With just five games of the season to go, Liverpool, who were top of the league, played Manchester City at Anfield, and Raheem played one of his best games yet. After just six minutes, he dribbled the ball into the City area, and Vincent Kompany, one of the best defenders in the world, came across to block him. Raheem stopped and looked up – and then, instead of passing the ball to Sturridge, who was running towards goal on his left, Raheem suddenly glided away to his right. He fooled everyone – Kompany, the City goalkeeper Joe Hart, even some of the people watching in the crowd – and, before anyone had the chance to look back in his direction, Raheem smashed the ball into the bottom corner of the net. 1–0!

Liverpool would go on to win the game 3–2, and the atmosphere afterwards in the city was as happy as a New Year's celebration. Could this be the year that they finally won the league again? They only had one very difficult game left, against Chelsea. They just needed to get a draw in that match, and the title was theirs.

But then Chelsea, whose manager was a very cunning man called José Mourinho, spoiled Liverpool's plan. Chelsea came to Anfield and made all of their players defend their goal. Trying to get through Chelsea's defence was like trying to run through a forest in the middle of the night – you couldn't find a way, anywhere you looked. Raheem and his teammates kept pushing, kept pushing, but then they got too impatient, and twice they stopped paying attention. And that's when Chelsea ran up the other end of the pitch and scored.

Chelsea 2, Liverpool 0. Liverpool's hope had turned to heartbreak. Ever since Raheem had started playing football, he had been desperate to win trophies: but now Manchester City were the champions, and his team was not.

THE GOLDEN BOY

Though Raheem was very sad that Liverpool did not win the league, it was still a good time for him. The club voted him as their Young Player of the Year for 2013–14, and he had played so well that football fans all across the world now knew who he was – and some of the most important people in the game were very, very impressed by what he was doing. A few months into the season, Liverpool received some wonderful news – Raheem had won an award called the Golden Boy, a trophy for the best young player in the whole of Europe!

Raheem was thrilled, as was his mum and the

rest of his family. They were just so happy to see all his hard work being rewarded. And to think that now he had won the same prize as players like Sergio Agüero, Wayne Rooney and Lionel Messi! Everything looked perfect for him.

But soon, everything changed.

Liverpool were very pleased with how Raheem was doing, and so they wanted to see if he would sign with them for a few years more. So, they offered him a lot of money, three times what he was earning. But Raheem said no.

Transfer Windows

A transfer window is a short period within the football season during which clubs can buy and sell players. FIFA (Fédération Internationale de Football Association) regulations set out two annual periods during which clubs can buy in players. The longer transfer window falls between seasons and the shorter one falls mid-season, but the exact timing is set by individual countries' football associations. Professional players sign contracts with clubs for a fixed term of up to five years. If a player transfers before their contract expires, the new club pays compensation to the old one. This is known as a transfer fee.

The Tide Turns

The club and many of the supporters were in shock. They couldn't understand. Things were going well, weren't they? Raheem's manager was as surprised as anyone. This was an incredible offer, he said. But Raheem had different ideas. He wanted to explain himself to the fans, and so he and his agent asked if they could do a television interview.

In the interview, Raheem said that he didn't turn down the contract because of the money. It wasn't about that, he said. What he cared about most was winning trophies. He would sign a long contract with the club where he had the biggest chance of winning.

If Raheem thought his TV interview would calm

things down, then he was wrong. It made many of Liverpool's fans even angrier than before.

"I don't believe Raheem! Of course it's about the money. He's just being greedy!"

"He's saying he hasn't got a good chance of winning at Liverpool? He's saying this club can't win trophies? Did we not just come close to winning the league?"

"What's he going on TV for? He should just keep quiet and concentrate on his football!"

The rest of the season would be hard for Raheem. Two of Liverpool's best players, Luis Suarez and Steven Gerrard, had left the club, and so that meant there was more pressure on Raheem to do well.

It was just too much. Liverpool finished the 2014–15 season in sixth place in the Premier League, all the way down from second, and Anfield no longer felt like home for Raheem. When Manchester City asked to buy him that summer, Liverpool said yes. And, after he sat down and discussed it with his family, so did Raheem.

A NEW START
FOR RAHEEM

Raheem's time at Liverpool had begun so well, but ended so badly. All he could do now was focus on life at his new club, and try not to think about what everyone was saying about him. Some people looked at what Manchester City had paid for him – 49 million pounds! – and said that he had cost too much. Was he really good enough, they asked, to be the most expensive English player in history?

There was too much noise around him, so Raheem just spent more time with his family. His girlfriend came to Manchester to be with him, and they soon had a daughter. His daughter didn't care about football yet, and so when he came home all the stress from his job went away. Now that he was happy at home, he started to play well again.

Manchester City

Club name: Manchester City Football Club
Nicknames: City, The Sky Blues
Founded: 1880
Current manager: Pep Guardiola
Current league: Premier League
Emblem: A golden ship, the red rose of Lancashire and three lines to symbolize the three rivers: the Irwell, the Irk and the Medlock

---

Raheem went straight into the team for the 2015– 2016 season, and three weeks after his arrival at City his first major achievement came. At home against Watford, with the score still 0–0, Raheem saw his teammate Bacary Sagna sprinting down the right wing. Raheem made a sprint of his own, into the penalty area, because he knew what was coming from Sagna – a low, curling cross, and as the ball dropped towards him Raheem, running nearly as fast as he could, put out his right foot. *1–0 City!* Raheem turned away from goal, and as the crowd roared he put his hands to his face in celebration. City ended up winning 2–0, their tenth win in a row, which was a club record. Could his start to life in Manchester get any better?

The answer: yes. Two months later, he scored his first hat-trick for City, getting three goals in a 5–1 win over Bournemouth. He also scored for them in the UEFA Champions League, helping them to finish ahead of Juventus, the mighty Italian team, in their qualifying group.

Yet after his brilliant arrival, Raheem's progress seemed to slow down. He was still working hard, but he was not as good as he had been in his early days. Maybe it was the pressure, maybe he was trying too hard, maybe he was unlucky; but, whatever the problem was, he stopped scoring goals.

His worst moment came when he went back to Anfield to play against Liverpool. All the love these fans once had for him had now turned to anger. They booed him every single time that he touched the ball: tens of thousands of people, together in their disapproval. Raheem was playing so badly that Manuel Pellegrini, the team's quiet but firm manager, decided to take him out of the team at half time. City lost 3–0, and Raheem had only scored once in his last twelve Premier League matches.

Many fans were very curious about why Raheem was no longer in the team. So were many journalists. Was he injured, they asked? No, said Mr Pellegrini. "There's not any reason. I just try and choose the best starting eleven for every game."

That made the journalists even more curious. If Raheem wasn't one of the best, did that mean he wasn't good enough to play for City? Did that mean he was a waste of money? The questions continued each week, and grew louder and louder.

Things would get better for Raheem at City. But before they did, they would have to get a lot worse.

SOMETHING VERY WORRYING

Right after Raheem's difficult first season for Manchester City, he was chosen to play for England, at the 2016 European Championships. England struggled through their first two games, drawing 1–1 with Russia and just beating Wales 2–1, and then drawing again with Slovakia, this time with a score of 0–0. Even though England had qualified for the next round, many of their fans were not happy. Their unhappiness had a big effect on some of the England players. And that is why, a few days before the next game against Iceland, something very worrying happened.

One afternoon Gary Neville, one of the senior coaches for the England football team, heard a knock on his office door. "Come in," he said. When the door opened he was surprised to see Raheem standing there, with the saddest look on his face. It was obviously something very important; he had never seen Raheem worried about anything. What could it be?

"Hey," said Raheem. "Have you got a minute? I just wanted to talk to you about something."

"Of course!" Gary rose from his seat and offered Raheem a chair next to his desk. "I have all the time you need."

Raheem didn't talk for a little while. He looked out of the window then down at his lap. "It's about the crowd," he said, still looking down. "The way they shout at me."

"But that's football," said Gary. "There's always some fans who will have a go at you." He thought back to one of England's recent games. "Look at the game against Wales, when the team came off at half-time. We weren't very good, and look – they booed everyone then."

"I know that, but this is different," said Raheem.

"It's more like – they boo me *all* the time. Not just when I mess up a pass, but when I am not even doing anything wrong. And sometimes the abuse even starts before the game. When I am warming up."

Gary couldn't believe what he was hearing.

"But Raheem, you're one of our best players," he said. "What on earth are they doing that for?"

"I just don't know," he said. He sounded so down.

"Raheem," said Gary, "you do know that we all love you to bits, don't you? Look at what you've done so far in your career. You are a great player and we are lucky to have you. Please never forget that. We all know how good you are. You're a great lad to have around."

"Thanks so much, Gary," said Raheem, but this only made Gary more concerned. He had seen one of Raheem's posts on Instagram a few days ago: he had posted a picture of himself with the hashtag #TheHatedOne.

"Raheem," said Gary, "just try your very best to block it out. Don't go online, don't listen to what people are saying. Just don't think about anything but getting on that pitch and showing everyone who you are. We are still in this tournament and you will have a big part to play for us, I am sure of it. Let's go, Raheem. Let's do this. We've got Iceland next. You're going to be big for us, I know it."

Raheem thanked Gary again and left, seeming a little happier, but Gary frowned as he watched him walk away. Neither man could imagine the storm that was just about to come.

England Backroom Staff

The key to a great team is not just to have amazing players on the pitch, but also to have a great team working together on the sidelines. In the build-up to the next World Cup in 2022, Gareth Southgate has a talented and supportive staff helping him to develop a winning team. The England coaching staff all bring outstanding personal qualities and experience of international football, which helps them to train and support the players.

In 2018, the PFA (the Professional Footballers' Association) launched a three-year programme placing BAME football coaches across all England teams, in conjunction with the FA. The scheme is designed to increase the visibility of BAME coaches and develop the coaching talent pool amongst black and minority ethnic coaches.

Former Three Lions defender Chris Powell joined Gareth's Southgate's senior men's coaching staff in September 2019 and will be part of the coaching staff during the 2019–2020 season through to the UEFA EURO 2020. As of September 2019, the England backroom staff includes:

Manager: Gareth Southgate
Assistant Manager: Steve Holland
Goalkeeping Coach: Martyn Margetson
Striker Coach: Allan Russell
Coach: Chris Powell
First-Team Doctor: Rob Chakraverty
Fitness Coach: Bryce Cavanagh
Physiotherapist: Steve Kemp

A CALL FROM PEP

"England's greatest humiliation," said the headlines of one newspaper. "Good riddance," said another. "A disgrace," said a third.

England had lost 2–1 to Iceland and they were out of the European Championships. It seemed like the whole country was in shock.

Alan Shearer, one of England's greatest strikers, said on TV, "That was the worst performance I have ever seen from an England team." Rio Ferdinand, one of England's greatest defenders, called it "embarrassing". England had 166 times as many people as Iceland. How could they lose to a team like that?

The fans were so angry, and a few hours later

they would get even angrier, this time at Raheem. The newspapers found pictures and videos on social media where Raheem was going around his house and showing people his nice cars and other expensive property. They said that Raheem cared more about money than about playing for his country. They called him selfish and arrogant.

The newspapers didn't know that the pictures and videos were taken of the house that Raheem had bought for his mum – a present to thank her for helping him so much his whole life. By the time most people knew this, it was too late. Raheem, in the eyes of many football fans, was already Raheem the Greedy.

There were plenty of reasons for him to be worried, but there was one huge reason to be hopeful.

Manchester City had appointed a new manager that summer, who would take over from Manuel Pellegrini, and his name was Pep Guardiola. Pellegrini had been very good at his job, but Pep was one of the greatest managers the game had ever seen. Most importantly, he really seemed to like Raheem.

One of the first things Pep Guardiola did that

summer, as soon as he got the job at City, was to call Raheem. Pep's words were a wonderful surprise.

"As long as you work for me," said Pep, "I will fight for you, so keep your head up and don't worry. I know you are a good player and you are a big part of my plans for next season."

Wow, thought Raheem, after they had finished speaking. *Wow. Pep Guardiola!* The man who'd won two Champions Leagues and three Spanish titles with Barcelona, and three German titles with Bayern Munich! The man who'd helped Lionel Messi to become one of the best players in the world? And now he was looking forward to working with Raheem?

The more he thought about this short chat with his new manager, the more excited Raheem felt about the upcoming season, and making a fresh start. Maybe next year really was going to be all right.

A LIGHT BLUE
STORM CLOUD

When the new season started in 2016, everyone was talking about Pep Guardiola, and no wonder. His City team were playing brilliant football – when they attacked, it was like a light blue storm cloud coming at you. They won their first six games of the league season, scoring eighteen goals and only letting in five. Some newspapers even started asking if they could go the whole season without losing a game.

Raheem was enjoying himself too, and he was playing better than ever before. He was scoring and making goals nearly every week, and he was so good that he was voted the best player in the Premier

League for the month of August. He could not be stopped, and neither could City.

And then they played Tottenham Hotspur.

Tottenham Hotspur – known as Spurs – had a manager called Mauricio Pochettino, and he was very, very clever. Pochettino knew that if you played against City, you couldn't wait for them to attack you. So he attacked City from the very start of the game, again and again, and that surprised them. By half time, Spurs were winning 2–0, and that was the final score.

Now that they had seen City lose, the other teams began to believe they could beat them too. And in December, just a few months later, big trouble came. First City lost 3–1 in their own stadium to Chelsea, and the next match they lost 4–2 to Leicester. No one was afraid of City any more. Three weeks later, they lost 1–0 to Liverpool, which pretty much ended their hopes of winning the league title. Now they were ten points behind Chelsea, the league leaders, and it wasn't even the New Year.

It had been a miserable Christmas for Raheem and his teammates, and they would not recover from it. They ended up losing the league by fifteen points to Chelsea. Even worse, they got knocked out of the FA Cup by Arsenal and beaten in the Champions League by Monaco, so they had no trophies at all. Supporters of different clubs were laughing at City. How could they spend all that money and still win nothing? The plan was for them to become the best club not only in Europe, but in the world – and they weren't even the best club in England!

For Pep, it was the first time as a manager that he had finished a season without a single medal to his name. When he was asked what he thought of his first twelve months in English football, he didn't hide his feelings. "A disaster," he said. This season, everybody had been ready and waiting to defeat his and Raheem's team – Liverpool, Chelsea, Manchester United, Spurs, Leicester. Next year, they would have to make sure that absolutely no one could prepare for what was coming next.

WORKING WITH PEP

"Raheem?" asked Pep, in a training session at the start of the 2017–18 season.

"Yes, boss?" answered Raheem.

"You see when someone passes you the ball? Don't control it with this part of your foot. Control it with the other part. With the inside, not the outside. You can do that, right?"

"Of course, boss."

"Good," said Pep. "Because when you control it with the outside, like you are doing at the moment, it gets stuck under your foot. That slows you down, and lets the defender catch you. And you are so fast that no defender should ever catch you."

"Thanks, boss," said Raheem, and thought, *He's right. But wow. This guy sees absolutely everything. How did he notice a small thing like that? When he talks to me, it's like I'm studying in the hardest class at school. It's like someone has turned my brain up to full power.*

Raheem loved working with Pep because his new boss dreamed about football even more than he did. Pep paid attention to everything – how his players were eating, how they were resting, how they were sleeping. He fussed over them like a mechanic fusses over expensive cars. And he wasn't scared of telling them if they couldn't do what he needed – if they couldn't do it, they would have to go, and the club would buy other players. Pep was very tough, but if he trusted you, you would play every week.

Raheem kept working hard, because he knew, though Pep trusted him, there were always new players who could take his place. He remembered those early days when his mum had told him not to go to Arsenal because he would meet fifty Raheems there who were just as good as him. Maybe those Raheems were out there somewhere right now, just waiting for him to slip up so they could play for City instead. Every time Pep talked, Raheem listened, he learned, he improved. It was like being eight years old again, turning up to those first few training sessions with Alpha and Omega, and trying to do his best for Clive and for his teammates.

Final Scorer

And so Raheem went out there and had his best season so far. He enjoyed the pressure; the closer he came to the other team's penalty area, the calmer he got. And that's when he started a habit: scoring very, very late in games, either to draw or win the match for his team.

The first time it happened, Everton had come to City's stadium, and they were winning by one goal to nil. City were trying everything, attacking the whole game, but it was all going wrong. All their shots were flying past the post and over the bar. The fans were groaning with worry, and Pep looked stressed too. He was walking up and down the side of the pitch like a man who was waiting to hear bad news from the doctor.

And then one of City's players hit the ball high

into Everton's area. An Everton defender tried to head the ball clear, but it fell straight to Raheem.

As Raheem watched the ball drop, he remembered every single lesson that Clive and Rodgers and Pellegrini and Pep and all his other coaches had ever taught him:

"Keep your eye on the ball."

"Move your body so when you kick the ball it goes towards the bottom corner. Goalkeepers find it very hard to save it when the ball goes there."

"Make sure you kick the ball with the front of your right foot, the part we call your laces."

"Once you've kicked the ball, keep swinging your right foot all the way through, that way you'll get the most power on your shot."

The ball fell, and Raheem swung his right foot at it. The cameras flashed; the crowd gasped; and the goalkeeper dived, but he didn't get close.

"Goooooooooooalllll," yelled the commentator. ""Goooooooooooalllll!" Everyone in the crowd went wild, and so did everyone on the City team, except for Raheem. He just jogged back to the halfway line, ready to start the game again. He leaned down, and pulled up his socks, and he looked as focused as he was when he caught that first bus to train with QPR.

City drew 1–1 against Everton, and they were so inspired by Raheem's goal that they went on to win the next game, and the next, and the next. Just like when Raheem was playing at Liverpool, the big victories came each week:

Manchester City 5, Liverpool 0!

Manchester City 6, Watford 0!

Manchester City 5, Crystal Palace 0!

Manchester City 7, Stoke City 2!

Manchester City 4, Swansea City 0!

The difference this time, though, was that there would be no painful defeats. Not this time. City just kept on going, and they won the title with more points than any team had achieved before. And Raheem kept on scoring, ending up with twenty-three goals in forty-six games. After so many years of hard work, after all that travel and all that sacrifice from everyone in his family, Raheem had finally done it. He was officially at the top.

SOMETHING STILL BOTHERS RAHEEM

Life was good for Raheem. He was a champion now, and playing better football than ever before – he was scoring and making goals almost every week, and Manchester City were top of the league. He and his girlfriend had a child, a son this time. He would often catch up with his mum and sister by phone – he didn't see them as much now, because they were still in London, but they were doing well.

But there was still something else that was bothering him. And finally, he decided that he had had enough.

He kept on seeing the same old stories in some of the newspapers and he was tired of it. Why did they always write about some footballers like they were just greedy people who only cared about themselves? Most of the footballers he knew were just like anyone else. They were very hardworking people who helped out their friends and families where they could. The only difference was that they were paid much more to do their jobs than most people were.

It wasn't all of the newspapers that were doing this – some journalists were very fair when they wrote about footballers – but it was a few of the most popular ones. They behaved like the biggest bullies in the playground. Some of them had been writing nasty things about Raheem for years, and so he was used to it. What he didn't like was that now they were being mean to some of the younger players, who were only just starting their careers. Raheem didn't think it was right that they were picking on them, and so one day he thought he would do something about it. Raheem didn't really like giving speeches – he wasn't one to talk much, it wasn't really his style. But he knew that now he was a famous footballer, more people were ready to listen to what he had to say.

Raheem wanted to talk about a big problem that he had seen in one newspaper. Two young players in his football team had done something very nice for their mums – they had bought them a house. When one player did this for his mum, the newspaper praised him, and said what a nice man he was. But when the other player did it, the newspaper said that someone as young as him shouldn't be spending all that money. The only difference between these players was that one player was white and the other player was black.

Raheem didn't think that was okay, and so he posted a photo of the newspaper on his Instagram account. Underneath the photo, he wrote a short message, saying that he didn't like the newspaper's behaviour. Both players were innocent, he wrote, and had just done something good for their families. But now the newspaper was trying to make the young black man look like a bad guy, which he wasn't. And that, wrote Raheem, was unacceptable.

In just a few hours, Raheem's Instagram post had tens of thousands of likes. It seemed as if everyone in football was talking about it. Journalists wrote long articles about it and it was the main subject on the news. In just a few weeks, the newspapers that were the biggest bullies changed how they wrote about

Raheem, and about some other black footballers. They realized that Raheem was too popular for them to pick on, and that if they kept picking on black players then their readers wouldn't like them so much.

Those newspapers were still mean now and then. But Raheem had stood up for what he thought was right, and he'd made people think about why the newspapers were mean to certain people but not others. Raheem had used his position as a famous footballer to make a positive change. He hoped that his mum, teachers, Clive, Pep and all the other people who had helped him during his career were proud of him.

TIME TO RELAX

It was the end of the season, and Raheem finally had time to relax.

He was famous for being one of the fastest footballers on the whole planet but that morning he was not even the fastest person in his own family. He was chasing his daughter round and round the house, but he couldn't catch her, and that was because there is absolutely nothing faster in the whole world than a naughty child. His daughter knew he was a superstar for Manchester City, but she didn't care. She knew who the best club in the whole world was.

"Liverpool!" she sang. "Liverpool!"

"Come back here," he shouted, trying to not to laugh.

"No!" she shouted. "Liverpool!" She ran round a corner, and by the time he got there, she had already disappeared.

In another room, Raheem's son was playing football. He was only small, but he could already kick the ball much harder than children who were three or four years older than him. When he saw Raheem walk into the room, his face shone with joy.

"Go on, score a goal," said Raheem, rolling the little blue ball towards him. His son rushed towards the ball and thrashed it with his right foot, sending it against the kitchen window.

"Whaaaat!" yelled Raheem, delighted.

"Gooalll!" yelled his son.

"Celebrate with me!" called Raheem, kneeling down and opening his arms. His son ran towards him, and they hugged. *Life is wonderful*, thought Raheem.

His mum was happy, living down in London in the house he had bought for her. His sister was happy, working in a career she really enjoyed. His girlfriend was happy, relaxing in the other room and smiling as he played with his children. And his season had come to a brilliant end. City had not only won the league again, they had also won the FA Cup and the Carabao Cup – and Raheem had scored in the finals of both games. He scored the winning penalty in the final of the Carabao Cup, and scored two goals in the FA Cup Final as City beat Watford by six goals to nil. Thanks to all his success, his fellow footballers voted him the best young player in the country.

This is the life, thought Raheem. He looked around and smiled. His family had always kept him going, and now he had a family of his own.

He knew that when he was surrounded by people who cared about him, people who wanted to be near him even when he was having the worst of days, there was nothing that could stop him. Look how far he had come. He had gone from the playgrounds of Wembley to being one of the best players in the world! What an incredible story – and it was only just beginning. Raheem couldn't wait to see where life would take him next.

What Makes Raheem Great?

Everyone agrees that Raheem is one of the best footballers in the world. He is a star for Manchester City, and a star for the England national team, who got all the way to the semi-final of the World Cup in Russia. He has won league championships and FA Cups. He has been voted the best footballer in the whole country.

But what is it that makes him so good?

To be a great player like Raheem, you have to be very good at plenty of different things, and Raheem is very good at six of them: pace, shooting, passing, dribbling, heading, and anticipation. Let's look at each of these things, one by one.

Pace

As a footballer, there are two main reasons why it's good if you have pace. The first reason is obvious: if two of you are running after a ball, then the quickest one — and that's normally Raheem — will get there first. The second reason is the most important: if you have pace, then you can surprise the other team when they are still getting ready to stop you.

In football, one of the best ways to score a goal is something called "the counter-attack", and Raheem is brilliant at it. The counter-attack works in a very clever way. It's like one of those nature programmes on TV when one animal, when it's trying to catch another animal, pretends to be asleep; and when the other animal comes too close, it jumps on them.

To counter-attack, you have to make a trap for the team you're playing against.

You do that by asking all of your own players to stand near your own penalty area, even your strikers, and then you organize them so that they defend very well. That way, the other team thinks, "Ah, this team doesn't want to score any goals, they just want to defend all day long."

So the other team starts to attack, and attack, and attack – but after they've tried for a while without scoring, they get tired and frustrated. They start sending more players forward, so now there are fewer and fewer people protecting their goal.

And that's when – once they start to lose their concentration – you send your fastest players to attack them. In a situation like this, the best passers on Manchester City's team – let's say, someone like Kevin de Bruyne or Bernardo Silva – will give the ball to Sergio Agüero, Leroy Sané or Raheem, and off they go.

In each of the last three years, Raheem has hit fifteen shots at goal after making a counter-attack. Only five other players in the whole of the Premier League have done that.

Another way in which Raheem uses his pace is when he is winning penalties. If you watch him, you will see that he speeds up as he reaches the penalty area. He goes so fast that defenders get desperate when they try to stop him, kicking him as he goes past. He has been given eleven penalties in the last three seasons – no player in the country has won more than that.

The other thing to note about Raheem's pace is how often he can use it. Most footballers can only run at full speed a few times each game; then, because this takes so much energy, they start slowing down. This is why the best teams score so many goals in the last few minutes of matches – because their opponents don't have the fitness to keep playing at that pace for the whole game.

But Raheem is relentless. Last season, he sprinted almost twenty times each match; he made a total of 666 sprints, and only three players had more than that.

If there was a Premier League title for speed, Raheem could win it.

Shooting

There was a time when many people said Raheem didn't score enough goals, and maybe they were right. They said that someone so quick, someone with so much skill, should be putting the ball in the net a lot more often. And so Raheem went away and worked on it, and the results were great.

Just look at how he much he improved. In his first

full season at Liverpool, Raheem scored two goals in thirty-six games, or one goal every eighteen games. In his most recent season, for Manchester City, he scored twenty-five goals in fifty-one matches, which is just under one goal every two games. Now, his manager even trusts him to take the final penalty in a penalty shootout, as Pep Guardiola did in the Carabao Cup Final against Chelsea.

The most impressive thing of all was how well he has done inside the penalty area, where his shooting is of a very high standard. In the 2018–2019 season, he took thirty-one shots in this area, and sixteen of them were on target.

He also scored seven goals inside the penalty area – more than anyone else in the Premier League, including brilliant strikers such as Mohamed Salah, Sergio Agüero and Harry Kane. To do this, he has mastered something very important, which is the art of movement – he is able to get away from defenders, so that he has room to shoot. Being good at shooting isn't just about having a hard shot, it's about getting the space to use it.

Raheem's success shows it is possible to make your game better each year. It is hard for people to imagine it now, but there was a time when Lionel Messi wasn't very good at taking free kicks. That was partly because he didn't really get to take them for Barcelona, but also because he was still practising his technique. At first, he scored one or two from free kicks each season, but these days he averages about seven goals from free kicks each year.

Another important thing to remember is that you don't have to be that big to have a powerful shot. When football fans look at someone like Raheem or Messi, they don't immediately think that they can kick the ball that hard. But shooting the ball well isn't always about having huge muscles in your legs – even though that helps. It is also about timing – about knowing exactly when to hit the ball, just when it bounces up, so that you can send it away with the greatest possible force.

So if you're in the same situation as Raheem – if you are small and don't score many goals, but you are still quick and have plenty of skill – then don't worry. There is so much that you can do to get better, and with just a few months of very hard work you will start to surprise yourself.

Passing

We don't expect players like Raheem to be very good at passing. If we watch their highlights videos on YouTube, we normally see them dribbling past one defender then another. When you are that good at running with the ball, why would you want to pass it?

But defenders in the Premier League, in the UEFA Champions League and at the World Cup are very clever. If they see the same attacker coming at them all the time, they can quickly work out how to stop them.

That is why attackers have to be excellent at what is called "associative play": or, in other words, passing well with your team-mates, and knowing where to move so they can pass to you with ease.

Recently, Raheem's associative play has been superb. In the last two seasons, he has been one of only three footballers in the Premier League to create twenty or more goals with his passing; and the only footballer to score more than thirty goals in the same time period. In fact, it can be argued that at the moment he is the best at associative play in the entire Premier League.

One reason why Raheem is so good at passing is that he is strong in other areas of his game. If defenders know that you can run fast, then they often stay further away from you, worried that you might sprint past them. That gives you more room to plan and make your passes.

Remember: the trick to being a great footballer is having so many different tools that the defenders never know which ones you are going to use, or when you are going to use them.

Dribbling

To be a brilliant footballer, one of the things you need to do is to surprise your opponents. Most of the time, they will have a plan to stop you from scoring, and it's your job to do things they are not prepared for.

If you're a player as famous as Raheem, then that's very difficult, because they will often have studied you for hours on video to see which movements you make on the field.

This is hardest of all when you are dribbling. Defenders will know which foot you prefer kicking with, they will know which skills you like to use most. But the very best dribblers, of which Raheem is one, understand something very well: that surprise lies not in the tricks you use, so much as when you use them.

Here's an example. If you are Raheem, and you are running towards a defender, the defender is thinking, "Here he comes, and most of the time when he dribbles he moves one particular way." The problem for the defender is that he doesn't know *when* you are going to make your move.

As a defender, you are always looking for clues to see where the attacker is trying to run, but Raheem's style of running doesn't give you any. Look at it – his back is straight, his shoulders are level with each other, and his arms are out to his sides. In football, that is what you call "balance" – it means that when the attacker changes direction at high speed they are almost impossible to stop.

How good is Raheem at dribbling? Well, in the 2018–2019 season he was one of only five players in the Premier League to dribble the ball past a defender more than eighty times; that's an average of over two successful attempts each match.

Heading

Raheem is not very tall, but he still scores several headed goals. In the 2018–2019 season, he scored as many goals with his head as Romelu Lukaku, a striker who is twenty centimetres taller than him. That is because, to be very good at heading, you don't always need to be big. You just need to know when to run for the ball, and when to jump.

In a game against Tottenham Hotspur in August 2019, Raheem scored the first goal with a header, and there was no one near him when he did it. Why was that? Because he made what football coaches call "a late run."

This is when the attacker stands a long way from goal when the ball is crossed in, and then – just before the ball lands in the area – the attacker sprints towards it. That way, when the defender is watching the ball, the attacker sneaks in behind him, and gets to it first. Raheem is so good at this that the defender doesn't see him coming.

Anticipation

As a footballer, there are three different ways that you can win the ball from your opponents. The first and the easiest, of course, is to wait until they kick it out of play. The second is by tackling them. And the third, and maybe the hardest, is the interception – which is when you see when one of their players is going to pass the ball to another, then steal it away with your feet before it gets there.

In the 2018–19 season, only four attackers in the Premier League had more interceptions than Raheem. That is because he is very good at anticipation, or being able to tell when the other team is going to make a mistake. Anticipation is a very special skill, because it means that you are always paying attention to what is happening – something that Raheem once got in trouble for not doing at school.

Why is it so good for attackers to make interceptions? Because if you do that, then you are through on goal, and their defenders are unprepared to stop you. They are getting ready to pass the ball down the field, and all of a sudden you have given them a problem they were not planning for.

But football is not only about numbers.

There is one other essential skill that Raheem has, and that is something called *versatility*. While some attackers can only play in one position, Raheem can play on the left wing, on the right wing, as an attacking midfielder and as a central striker. It takes very different skills to play on the wing than to play in the middle of the pitch.

If you play in the middle of the pitch it is much more crowded, so you have to think faster, because you have less time to use the ball before you get tackled. If you play on the wing, you have more space to run, but it can be harder to affect the game when you are on the edge of it. Raheem's ability to do both of these things is very useful to his coach. Why is that useful? Because it means that if another player gets injured, Raheem can fill their spot, and the team will still play very well.

Most importantly, Raheem is a great teammate. Being part of a successful football team is like being part of a happy family – everyone has to make a big effort to help each other, every day. Sometimes helping each other isn't always exciting, or even fun, but you still have to do it. Raheem is a star because he keeps running, he keeps attempting the best passes, keeps trying to win games for his team. He never gives up, and that, more than anything else, is what makes him great.

With thanks to Opta for providing the information for this chapter.

Raheem Sterling Timeline

8 December 1994   Raheem Sterling is born in Kingston, Jamaica.

1996   Raheem's father is killed when Raheem is just two years old

30 June 1998   England go out of the World Cup in France after losing on penalties to Argentina.

1999   At the age of five, Raheem emigrated to London with his mother.

2000   Raheem meets Clive Ellington when he is 8 years old. He spends four years with local youth team Alpha & Omega.

2004	Raheem joins the QPR Academy at the age of ten.
1 July 2006	England go out of the World Cup in Germany on penalties in their quarter-final against Portugal.
5 November 2009	Raheem first represents England at Under-16 level against Northern Ireland.
27 February 2010	15-year-old Raheem joins Liverpool for a fee of £600,000.
27 June 2010	England crash out of the World Cup in South Africa, losing 4–1 to Germany in the round of sixteen.
14 February 2011	Raheem scores five goals in a 9–0 win over Southend in the FA Youth Cup.
24 February 2011	Raheem receives his first call up to the senior team for the away-leg of the Europa League match against Sparta Prague.
14 November 2012	Raheem makes his senior debut for England, starting in a friendly away to Sweden.

24 March 2012	Raheem makes his debut for the Liverpool first team in a home League game against Wigan.
13 May 2012	Manchester City win the Premier League, their first league title since 1968.
1 June 2012	Brendan Rodgers is unveiled as the new Liverpool manager.
2 August 2012	Raheem makes his European debut for Liverpool.
12 August 2012	Raheem nets his first senior strike in his first home start for the Reds in a friendly against Bayer Leverkusen.
23 August 2012	Raheem makes his first competitive start for Liverpool away to Hearts in the Europa League.
26 August 2012	Raheem makes his first start in a Premier League match in a 2–2 draw against Manchester City at Anfield.

10 September 2012	Raheem is called up to the senior England squad for the first time for a 2014 World Cup qualifying match against Ukraine, where he was an unused substitute.
15 September 2012	Raheem is named Liverpool's man of the match in a 1–1 draw with Sunderland.
20 September 2012	Raheem travels to Switzerland to play Young Boys in a UEFA Europa League group match. Liverpool win 5–3.
October 2012	Raheem is called up for the first time to the England Under-21 squad and makes his debut as a substitute during a match against Serbia on 16 October.
20 October 2012	Raheem scores his first competitive goal for Liverpool, netting the winner in a 1–0 victory over Reading.
21 December 2012	Raheem signs a new five-year contract with Liverpool.

2012	Raheem's daughter, Melody Rose Sterling, is born.
27 January 2013	Raheem plays in the Liverpool FA Cup 4th round tie away against Oldham, becoming Liverpool's youngest ever FA Cup player.
13 May 2013	Manchester City's manager, Roberto Mancini, is fired.
14 June 2013	Manuel Pellegrini is confirmed as Manchester City's new manager.
13 August 2013	Raheem scores his first goal for England Under-21 squad in a 6–0 win against Scotland.
5 March 2014	Raheem earns his second cap and is named man of the match as England beat Denmark 1–0.
18 April 2014	Raheem is named as one of the six players on the shortlist for the PFA Young Player of the Year award.
27 April 2014	Chelsea beat Liverpool 2–0, ruining the Reds' chances of winning the Premier League. Manchester City win the cup.

6 May 2014	Raheem is named Liverpool's Young Player of the Year.
8 May 2014	Raheem is named Liverpool Chartered Player of the Month for April.
11 May 2014	Manchester City win the Premier League with a 2–0 victory over West Ham.
June 2014	England fail to qualify from the group stage at the World Cup in Brazil.
31 August 2014	Raheem scores the opening goal in a 3–0 league win against Tottenham at White Hart Lane and is named man of the match.
16 September 2014	Raheem makes his UEFA Champions League debut in a 2–1 victory over Bulgarian champions Ludogorets Razgrad.
23 September 2014	Raheem is named the Liverpool Player of the Month for August.

9 December 2014	Liverpool are eliminated from the 2014–15 UEFA Champions League and drop into the Europa League after drawing 1–1 with Basel at Anfield.
January 2015	Raheem is given a break from playing. He uses this time off to holiday in Jamaica.
27 March 2015	Sterling scores his first senior goal for England in a 4–0 UEFA Euro 2016 qualifier against Lithuania.
1 April 2015	Raheem turns down a £100,000-a-week Liverpool deal.
16 April 2015	For the second year in a row, Raheem is named as one of the six players on the shortlist for the PFA Young Player of the Year award.
19 May 2015	Raheem is named Liverpool's Young Player of the Year.
14 July 2015	Raheem completes his move to City, for a fee of up to £49,000,000, making him the most expensive English player in history at the time.

10 August 2015	Raheem plays in his first game for City with a 0–3 win away to West Bromwich Albion.
29 August 2015	Raheem scores his first competitive goal for Manchester City in a 2–0 win against Watford.
17 October 2015	Raheem scores his first career hat-trick at City, beating Bournemouth 5–1.
3 November 2015	Raheem scores his first UEFA Champions League goal in a 3–1 win away to Sevilla.
8 December 2015	On his 21st birthday, Raheem scores twice in City's last group stage fixture against Borussia Mönchengladbach.
1 February 2016	Pep Guardiola signs as Manchester City's new manager.
1 July 2016	England lose 2–1 to Iceland and crash out of the European Championship.
9 September 2016	Raheem wins EA SPORTS Player of the Month award for August.

15 March 2017	Manchester City lose 3–1 to Monaco and crash out of UEFA Champions League.
23 April 2017	Manchester City lose 2–1 to Arsenal and are knocked out of the FA Cup.
21 May 2017	Chelsea win the Premier League cup with City trailing 15 points behind.
2017	Raheem's son, Thiago, is born.
13 May 2018	Manchester City win the Premier League.
12 August 2018	Raheem scores the opening goal in Manchester City's 2–0 away win against Arsenal. The strike is Sterling's 50th Premier League goal.
4 November 2018	Raheem scores twice in a 6–1 win against Southampton, scoring his 50th goal for Manchester City in all competitions.
24 February 2019	In the Carabao Cup Final against Chelsea, Raheem scores the winning penalty to win the cup.

22 March 2019	Raheem scores his first hat-trick for England in a 5–0 win over the Czech Republic in a UEFA Euro 2020 qualifier.
4 August 2019	In the 2019 FA Community Shield against Liverpool, Raheem scores the opening goal of the match. Manchester City win the title 5–4 on penalties.
10 August 2019	Raheem scores a second-half hat-trick – his third of the calendar year – in a 5–0 away win over West Ham.
22 October 2019	Raheem scores his first UEFA Champions League hat-trick in a 5–1 win over Atalanta.

Raheem's Clubs

Queens Park Rangers

Club name: Queens Park Rangers Football Club
Nickname: The Super Hoops
Short name: Rangers
Founded: 1882
Current manager: Mark Warburton
Current league: Championship League
Emblem: A circular crest with the club's initials

Liverpool

Club name: Liverpool Football Club
Nickname: The Reds
Founded: 1892

Current manager: Jürgen Klopp
Current league: Premier League
Emblem: The Liver Bird, an imaginary cross between an eagle and a cormorant, with the words "You'll never walk alone"

Manchester City

Club name: Manchester City Football Club
Nickname: The Sky Blues
Short name: City
Founded: 1880
Current manager: Pep Guardiola
Current league: Premier League
Emblem: A golden ship, the red rose of Lancashire and three lines to symbolize the three rivers: the Irwell, the Irk and the Medlock

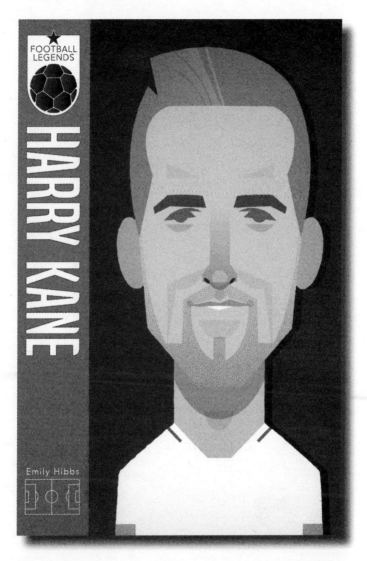

FOOTBALL
LEGENDS

HARRY KANE

Emily Hibbs

If you loved reading about **Raheem Sterling**,
why not read about **Harry Kane** next?

KANE'S
FIRST KICKS

Harry Edward Kane was born on 28 July 1993 at Whipps Cross Hospital, London, just five miles down the road from White Hart Lane, Tottenham Hotspur's home stadium. Harry's mum, Kim, was an assistant at a dental practice and his dad, Pat, owned a garage. Kim and Pat were loving and supportive, and Harry's big brother, Charlie, was his best friend growing up. The Kanes were a family of football fanatics and huge Spurs fans.

Almost as soon as he could walk, Harry was toddling down to the local park with Pat and Charlie for a kickabout. The small playing field wasn't exactly a world-class stadium. There were no nets or markings, and certainly no cheering crowds, but the trio made do with a patch of grass and a couple of trees for goalposts.

Harry quickly became as obsessed with football as the rest of his family, and a highlight of the week was going to see Spurs play at White Hart Lane. At his first match, four-year-old Harry sat in the crowd, proudly wearing his white-and-blue Spurs shirt, spellbound by the incredible players racing around the field below him. His favourite player, striker Teddy Sheringham, had just transferred to Manchester United. But as one of Tottenham's all-time highest goalscorers he was still Harry's hero, and his preferred footballer to copy at the park. After watching a match, Harry and Charlie practised the tricky tackles and skilful finishes they'd seen at the Lane.

A Sporting Start

When Harry was six the family moved to nearby Chingford, hometown of another legendary footballer, David Beckham. Harry dreamed of following in David's footsteps and becoming a sporting star himself, so when he spotted an advert for a trial at Ridgeway Rovers, the local club that David played for when he was a boy, Harry knew he had to go for it.

At the warm-up, the coach of Ridgeway Rovers, Dave Bricknell, introduced himself to the ten boys hoping to join his team and asked if anyone was up for having a go in goal. Harry preferred scoring goals to saving them, but he was keen to show the coach that he was happy to do anything, so he put his hand in the air to volunteer. Harry played well as a goalkeeper, making some skilful saves, and Dave was impressed. But then someone suggested that he should try Harry on the pitch – it turned out he was even better on the field than he was between the posts. Harry ran around the training ground, scoring goals from way down the field.

The trials were a success. Every week, Kim or Pat drove Harry to the nearby training ground, where he worked on improving his technique and building up his strength. He soon became Ridgeway Rovers' number-one striker.

Rubbing Shoulders with Rivals

Ridgeway Rovers had lots of strong players. Scouts from bigger clubs often came to watch their matches. Less than a year after Harry had joined the team, a scout invited him to a trial session for the youth academy of a Premier League club – it wasn't Harry's beloved Spurs, but their rivals, Arsenal! Still, the opportunity to play for such a strong team was too good to miss. Compared to Ridgeway Rovers' training ground, Arsenal's facilities were state-of-the art, with pristine pitches, gyms and meeting rooms.

Academy Trials

Big clubs like Arsenal and Tottenham Hotspur do not offer open trials. Instead, the clubs send out scouts, people whose job it is to search for talented players from local teams. Once a scout has spotted a player they think the club might be interested in, they make a recommendation, and the academy coaches might invite that player to a trial. At the trials, coaches look for players that can fill gaps in their current line-up, as well as someone with a strong technique and a personality that will fit in with the team.

Harry performed well at the trials and signed up with Arsenal for a whole season. He made the most of every opportunity, and though he wasn't as fast as some of the other boys, his powerful shots often found their mark. At the end of the season, however, there was bad news. On a walk to the park together, Pat put a hand on Harry's shoulder. "I've got to tell you something," he said. "Arsenal have released you." It meant that he wouldn't be continuing at the club. The coaches didn't think he was athletic enough and were worried about his pace.

Harry was disappointed. He'd done his best for the academy, even though his heart belonged to another club, and they had still decided to let him go.

But Pat wasn't fazed, he told Harry that if they worked hard, he'd be chosen to play for another club soon enough.

Embarrassing Photo

Years later, when Harry was playing for Tottenham, Arsenal fans found an old photo of him wearing the Gunners' kit at the academy and shared it on the internet. They thought the photo proved Harry wasn't a true Spurs fan. But Harry hit back at his critics, saying, "I wanted to wear a Tottenham kit but I don't think that would've gone down too well. I was eight years old . . . I just wanted to play football."

Coming soon!

Be inspired by more Football Legends.

Two new titles available September 2020